Original title:
Tasting the Sweetness

Copyright © 2025 Creative Arts Management OÜ
All rights reserved.

Author: Jude Lancaster
ISBN HARDBACK: 978-1-80586-426-4
ISBN PAPERBACK: 978-1-80586-898-9

Candles and Confections

With icing on my nose, I grin,
A cupcake's fight, oh let's begin!
The sprinkles dance, the frosting swirls,
Oh, how it tempts us silly girls.

A candle lit upon the cake,
I blow so hard, the flames all shake.
My wishes scatter, one by one,
Perhaps a sweet tooth is just fun!

Fragrant Tastes of Tomorrow

Tomorrow's treats wrapped up in bows,
Eclairs and pies, oh how it shows!
The scent of cookies fills the air,
I'm here to snack, so don't you dare!

The dough it rises, puffs with glee,
I'd race the chaffinch for a spree.
With every bite, I laugh and sing,
This sweet delight is just my thing!

Gentle Sips of Solace

A milky shake with extra cream,
I take a sip, I almost scream!
Chocolate swirls and fruit galore,
The blender's song, I can't ignore.

With every gulp, a silly face,
I spill so much, it's quite the case.
But laughter bubbles, joy unfolds,
In these moments, life consoles.

Serenade of the Sweets

Oh, lollipop, you're such a tease,
I lick, I laugh, I do it with ease.
The jelly beans, they start to sing,
A sugary tune, what joys they bring!

Macarons dancing on my plate,
Each polite bite, oh, isn't fate!
With sugar highs, we twirl and sway,
This serenade makes all things play.

Euphoria on the Tongue

A jelly bean parade in my mouth,
Dancing licorice, never a drought.
Fudge drips like a summer storm,
    Candy statues, oh so warm.

Chocolate rivers flowing wide,
Gummy bears, in sugar we ride.
Every bite's a laugh out loud,
Sweet dreams, no need to be cowed.

Cotton candy clouds above,
With marshmallow fluff, who needs love?
Jelly tots and lemon drops,
With every nom, my heart just hops.

Bitter greens, no thank you please,
I'm here for fun, my taste buds tease.
Life's too short for just plain toast,
Bring on the sweets, I'll raise a toast!

A Symphony of Delightful Bites

Biscuit balls drum a tasty beat,
Nuts in helmets march down the street.
Jelly rolls spin like dancers do,
Every nibble brings giggles too.

Cupcakes wearing frosting crowns,
Popcorn kernels throw their gowns.
Ice cream waltzes in a cone,
Each scoop's absurdity is well-known.

Bananas with a goofy grin,
Whipped cream whirls as we begin.
Syrup rivers flow with flair,
Every flavor leaves a glare.

In this feast, we lose all shame,
Devouring bites like it's a game.
Chocolate chips that wink and mock,
In this silliness, I'll gladly rock!

Floating on Blueberry Clouds

Pancakes stack like laughs on high,
Syrupy sweetness lifts me to the sky.
Waffles grin with crispy flair,
Blueberry bombs burst without care.

Frogs in jelly jump and play,
Marshmallows cloud the light of day.
Berries swim in cream so thick,
Life's a joke, and I'm the pick.

Sugar sprinkles like rain from above,
Take a bite, I'm in sweet love.
Sunny zest on every tongue,
Bubblegum blowout, joy's just begun.

Taste the fun in every bite,
Let candy dreams take flight tonight.
In this moment, I'm a child anew,
Floating on clouds, with skies so blue!

Lollipops in Twilight

In twilight's glow, kids make a dash,
Chasing flavors, a candy smash.
A lollipop's swirl, a rainbow's bend,
Giggles and sugar, a sweet weekend.

With sticky fingers and smeared cheeks wide,
A grape explosion, they cannot hide.
Their laughter echoes under the moon,
As chocolate dreams make mischief bloom.

Tastebuds Awakened

A jellybean jumps, it's a wild delight,
Wobbling along, causing quite a fright.
The orange ones dance, the berry ones roll,
While cotton candy clouds make them lose control.

Beneath the sun with every bright scoop,
Marshmallow monsters join the crazy troupe.
A party of flavors, a confection parade,
Oh, the silly dances that the sugar made!

The Golden Elixir

A bottle of sunshine, oh what a find,
Sweet nectar swirls, tickling the mind.
Sipped with a straw, it shoots like a dart,
A giggle eruption, that's just the start.

Golden elixirs take over the scene,
Where each drop's laughter falls like confetti gleam.
A fizz and a pop, a wiggly cheer,
It bubbles and giggles, spreading good cheer!

Nature's Sugary Kiss

Honeybees buzz, dancing through air,
Gathering sweetness, without a care.
A spoonful of nectar drips with a smile,
Turning grim faces into laughter's style.

Plucking ripe berries, a mischievous game,
Staining their fingers, oh what a shame!
With nature's love, they wander and roam,
Creating a kingdom of sweetness at home.

The Bounty of Sweetened Dawn

Morning's sugar-coated light,
Birds perform with pure delight.
Coffee spills, a sticky mess,
Who knew breakfast could impress?

Pancakes flip, they dance and twirl,
Syrup drips, a sweetened whirl.
Butter laughter, joy in cream,
Mornings burst like a sweet dream.

Flavorful Echoes of Laughter

Lemon drops in every joke,
Giggles rise with cherry smoke.
Candy colors paint the air,
Sugar rush, a light affair.

Gummy bears on every side,
In this laughter, we confide.
Like marshmallows in a stew,
Life's a treat, and so are you.

Confectionery Secrets in the Breeze

Cotton candy swirls around,
Secrets whispered, flavors found.
Chocolate whispers in our ears,
Marshmallows bounce, igniting cheers.

Frosted dreams float in the air,
Silly grins, and laughter rare.
Every bite a playful tease,
Joy unwrapped like fresh-baked sweets.

Candied Memories Unfolding

Nostalgia tastes like bubblegum,
Tickles funny bones, oh what fun!
Sprinkles dance upon the cake,
Every smile, a joy to make.

Chocolate rivers, laughter flows,
Hidden treats, nobody knows.
Life's a party, sweet and bright,
Candied memories take their flight.

Embracing the Flavorful

In a kitchen where mishaps reign,
A blender dances, causing a strain.
Spilled sugar, what a clumsy spree,
Sugar ants throw a wild jubilee!

Pies are laughably lopsided,
Cakes that look like they've collided.
Yet every bite brings a hearty cheer,
With giggles shared and desserts near.

Chocolate fountains with wobbly streams,
Dunking snacks in gooey dreams.
Laughter bubbles with every slip,
A delightful, chaotic friendship trip!

So here's to flavors, bold and free,
With every blunder, there's glee!
Life's sweetest moments often bend,
Let's embrace them, my dear friend!

Essence of the Orchard

In the orchard, apples play tag,
With pears whispering, 'Don't lag!'
The sun shines down, a comedic spark,
As squirrels barter for treats in the park.

Bananas slip on peels galore,
While grapefruits roll, daring to explore.
Overripe cherries giggle with pride,
As they bounce in a berry brigade ride.

Fruit flies laughing, gathering round,
To witness the craziest flavors found.
A picnic blanket becomes a stage,
As fruits join in a fruity rage!

So gather your snacks, make a cheer,
Each bite of juiciness, oh so dear!
In this orchard of joy, what can we find?
A feast of funny fruits, oh how kind!

Luxuries of the Tastebud

Oh, behold the gala of flavors so bright,
Cupcakes wearing hats, what a silly sight!
Marshmallows frolic with sprinkles in tow,
As jellybeans dance, putting on a show.

Macarons whisper, 'Join the elite,'
While donuts declare, 'We can't be beat!'
A tastebud ball with laughter and cheer,
Food critics snickering, 'What's the next beer?'

Caramels glide, oh so suave,
As cookies jam with a groovy suave.
The flavors collide, what a hilarious chase,
As tastebud royals take their place.

In this banquet of humor, let's all partake,
Each dish brings laughter to both fools and the great.
The secrets of pleasure, they always unfurl,
In the luxury of laughter, let's twirl!

A Feast of Indulgence

Gather 'round, it's a feast for the bold,
With chicken that dances and hot dogs sold!
Pickles take turns, swaggering around,
While ketchup tries out a circus sound.

Burgers sporting toppings galore,
Each one declaring, 'I can offer more!'
A bun that sings with each juicy bite,
As lettuce does flips, oh what a sight!

Mashed potatoes twirl like a waltz,
As gravy slicks back, not a single fault.
The rolls are joined by butter's embrace,
As everyone shouts, 'This is the place!'

Gorging on laughter, we merrily dine,
With every bite, life's worries decline.
So here's to the feasts that make us all grin,
Where fun meets flavor, let the joyful begin!

Candied Memories

In the jar, gumdrops collide,
A jellybean slip, oh what a ride!
Sticky fingers and laughing loud,
Sweets unite us, we feel so proud.

Chocolate rivers, who does that flow?
Marshmallow clouds in a sugary show.
We taste the past with every bite,
Wacky memories making things light.

Licorice ropes tied in knots,
Who knew sugar could create such plots?
With every nibble, we giggle and cheer,
Sweet moments mixed with childhood near.

From candy canes to tart lollipops,
Each bite ignites joyful hops.
A sprinkle of laughter, a dash of fun,
In the land of sweets, we all have won.

The Comfort of Sweetness

A donut here and a cookie there,
Chocolate frosting smeared in my hair!
Laughter erupts as we munch away,
Sugar smiles brighten the day.

Cupcakes tower, frosting galore,
Who could eat just one? Who knows what's in store!
Sighs of pleasure with each gooey bite,
In the kingdom of sweets, everything's right.

Gummy bears dance on the floor,
Chasing each other, what's in store?
With every chew, a burst of delight,
Making us chuckle until late at night.

When life feels heavy, just take a scoop,
Of ice cream dreams and a sugary loop.
These moments together, forever we'll cheer,
In a universe sweet, there's always good beer!

Fruity Reverie

Banana peels slip as we run,
Pineapple laughter, oh what fun!
Juicy slices, we can't resist,
With every fruit, we laugh and twist.

Watermelon seeds fly far and wide,
As we giggle and jump, side by side.
Tangy citrus, zesty and bright,
Tickling our tongues, what a silly sight!

Berry frenzy, a little tart taste,
Nibbles of goodness; we're never in haste.
Sticky hands reaching for more,
Fruity adventures that we adore!

In the orchard, we scamper around,
Tripping on peaches, we fall to the ground.
With fruity delight and giggles galore,
These playful moments, we couldn't ask for more!

The Symphony of Sugar

Sweets play a tune, a sugary song,
Candy canons firing, oh so strong!
Licorice violins play a sweet slide,
With gummy bears dancing side by side.

Every note is a sprinkle of fun,
Chocolate symphonies for everyone!
Lollipops twirling in a sugary waltz,
Making us giggle, no need for halts.

Marshmallow flutes join the parade,
In this candy fest, we aren't afraid.
Bubbles of laughter fill the air,
As we sing along without a care.

So grab a cupcake and join the chorus,
In this sweet world, it's glorious!
Together we'll ride this delightful wave,
In the symphony of sugar, we'll forever save!

Drying Flowers and Honey

A flower's perfume fills the air,
Like dessert, it's beyond compare.
With bees that buzz and dance around,
They wear their pollen like a crown.

Sunshine drips from jars so bright,
Sticky fingers, what a sight!
Petals wilt, but not the taste,
In nature's kitchen, none go to waste.

A spoonful here, a drizzle there,
Swatting flies without a care.
Laughter blossoms in the gloom,
As sweet escapes fill up the room.

So grab a snack, join the cheer,
With honeyed grins, spread the cheer.
Life's a treat, let's take a bite,
With flowers dried, it feels just right!

A Journey Through Delight

On a path of treats we roam,
With cupcakes leading us back home.
A jellybean's a friendly scout,
It pulls us in, no need to pout.

Chocolate rivers, fudgey streams,
We float away on candy dreams.
Gummy bears and licorice trails,
Giggles follow, neverFails.

A sprinkle here, a twirl of fun,
Life's a party; it's just begun.
With every step, there's joy to find,
A journey sweetens, hearts aligned.

So come along, let's run and play,
In this world of treats today.
No map required, just take a bite,
Adventure awaits, pure delight!

Swirls of Joy

A cone of ice, so creamy, bright,
It melts away, but feels just right.
Sprinkles dance like tiny stars,
As laughter floats to Mars and Bars.

Marshmallow clouds in the sky above,
Whipped up sweetness, we can't help but love.
With flavors swirling, oh so bold,
Each scoop is magic; a thrill untold.

Grab a spoon, or just dig in,
Here we go with a cheeky grin.
With every lick, there's laughter's sound,
A sugary joy we've newly found.

So let's all twirl, let's all scream,
In this candy-coated dream.
Swirls of joy, let's shout hooray,
For sweetness reigns at least today!

Melodies of Marshmallow

In a land where marshmallows take flight,
They bounce and giggle, what a sight!
Singing songs on candy clouds,
Making friends with lollipop crowds.

A frosty tune, a sugary beat,
With gummy bears tapping their feet.
Fudge echoes from valleys near,
As chocolate bars lend an ear.

Each fluff a note, each bite a rhyme,
Chasing joy, having a great time.
Caramel whispers sweet serenades,
In confectionery charades.

So join this choir, let it soar,
With flavors joined at every door.
In melodies of marshmallow delight,
Every giggle feels just right!

The Nectar of Serenity

Oh, honey drips from every bee,
Wobbling like a jelly spree.
Grab a spoon, don't be shy,
It's a sticky, sweetened pie!

Laughter bubbles in the jar,
Like sugar from a candy car.
Sipping syrup, goofy grins,
Who knew sweetness came with spins?

Gummy bears in wild delight,
Dancing with the sugar sprite.
Catch the taste, it's quite absurd,
A flavor chaos, oh, so blurred!

With a cake that leaps and flies,
Frosting dreams in big, wide skies.
Every bite a chuckle loud,
Spreading joy like a sweet crowd!

Exploring Sweet Realms

In candy lands where giggles reign,
Chocolate rivers, oh what a gain.
Lollipops twirl as we explore,
Each bite whispers, 'Come back for more!'

Marshmallow clouds float in the air,
Fudge mountains, if you dare.
A sprinkle fight, oh what a sight,
Sugar wars from morning till night!

Gumdrops bounce like happy bees,
Frosting floods and sugary trees.
Candy critters join in the play,
In this sweet realm, there's no gray!

Laughter echoes in candy lanes,
With giggles pouring like sweet rains.
Join the fun, don't miss the chance,
In this land of sugary dance!

A Palette of Pleasures

A brush of candy paints the day,
Sundae swirls in a vibrant display.
Sprinkles rain on our delight,
Creating flavors, oh what a sight!

Caramel's swirl, a dreamy hue,
Like a sweet bazaar just for you.
Taste the giggles from every sip,
Delight spills out with each little dip!

Pudding puddles by the stream,
Where every dessert fulfills a dream.
Cupcake towers, frosted cheer,
Making funny faces, oh so clear!

Swinging spoons with messy flair,
Painted smiles in the sweetened air.
A palette bright, it's all a joke,
In this candy land, we happily poke!

Slices of Joy

Slice of cake, giggle slice,
Cheesecake winks, oh so nice.
Gather round, let's have a feast,
With every bite, laughter's the beast!

Fruit by the slice, a juicy game,
Watermelon smiles, who's to blame?
Each chop brings a silly cheer,
Squirting juices, oh dear, oh dear!

Cupcake tops that wobble high,
Frosting fights make spirits fly.
In every nibble, a giggle waits,
Creating moments on our plates!

Choco chunks in a silly dance,
Cookies falling, given a chance.
Share these slices with a grin,
In laughter's sweetness, let's begin!

A Canvas of Flavor

A pickle danced with chocolate cheer,
While jellybeans sang loud and clear.
Cookie monsters made a grand parade,
Their frosting hats were all displayed.

A donut tried to juggle sprinkles,
But ended up in awkward crinkles.
Syrup rivers flowed with glee,
As pancakes stacked up to the sea.

Peanut butter played hide and seek,
With jelly giggling at its peak.
A pie took flight, a plate on wings,
Oh, the joy that pastry brings!

So grab a fork, give it a whirl,
In this flavorful, fun-filled swirl.
Let laughter rise with every taste,
In this canvas where flavors are chased.

Sugary Dreams at Dusk

Marshmallows bounced on fluffy clouds,
While gummy bears cheered in sweet crowds.
Cotton candy swirled up high,
Chasing moonbeams in the sky.

Cupcakes wore their sprinkles proud,
With frosting faces, oh so loud.
Chocolate rivers flowed like dreams,
In the land of sugary schemes.

Lollipops danced with great delight,
While chips made jokes in the moonlight.
Cookies whispered, 'Join the fun!'
As dreams of sugar come undone.

So let your laughter fill the night,
With every sweet, a new delight.
In sugary dreams, we all will play,
As dusk brings joy, come what may.

Whimsy in Every Bite

A pizza twirled in ballet shoes,
While pasta giggled with the blues.
Carrots juggled, peas took a stroll,
In this kitchen, laughter is the goal.

A sandwich posed, oh what a sight,
With a pickle bowtie, dressed just right.
Mashed potatoes joined in the fun,
And gravy flowed till day was done.

Tacos sang in harmony sweet,
While nachos danced with two left feet.
Chips had a party, salsa on deck,
Each bite a joke, a culinary wreck.

So come and join this vibrant show,
With whimsy in every bite you know.
Where food is fun, and palates cheer,
In this comedy feast, bring good cheer!

Edible Euphoria

A burger grinned beneath a crown,
With pickles bright, it won the town.
Fries marched on, a savory troop,
In this land of a tasty loop.

Sushi rolled with the grace of a drum,
While noodles giggled, 'Here we come!'
A salad tossed with flair so wild,
This feast is like a happy child.

Brownies winked under the lights,
While cupcakes planned their sweet delights.
Whipped cream clouds floated on high,
As laughter seeped into the sky.

So come partake in this great spree,
Where joy is served, come taste with me.
In edible euphoria, we find our place,
With every bite, a smiling face.

Palate's Pleasures

In the land of jelly beans, so bright,
Gummy bears dance with pure delight.
Chocolate rivers flow like a stream,
Candy canes twirl, oh what a dream!

Marshmallow clouds hang in the air,
Fruits in hats, what a silly affair.
Swedish fish swim in fizzy pop,
With lollipops that never will stop!

Syrup rivers sticky and sweet,
Donut trees serve a frosted treat.
Laughing spices in a kooky mix,
Taste buds giggle, doing silly tricks!

So gather round for a sugary feast,
Where every nibble is a joyful beast.
With every munch and every crunch,
Life's like a never-ending lunch!

Bites of Bliss

Take a bite of this, a nibble and grin,
Cotton candy clouds, let the fun begin!
Peanut butter pools where jellyfish swim,
Cake pops rolling like a sweetened whim!

Fruity loops flying in the bright blue sky,
Lemonade rivers with a twist of hi-fi.
A cookie monster giggles in glee,
Half-baked muffins dancing, oh so free!

Crispy crackers sing with crunch around,
Fudge fountains bubble with a wobbly sound.
In this world of munchies, laughter is key,
Bites of joy, come join the spree!

With every gulp, and a slurp or two,
Silly whispers and giggles brew.
A bash of flavors in a quirky twist,
Here's to moments that we can't resist!

A Harvest of Happiness

In orchards ripe where fruits collide,
Peaches in hats make me laugh inside.
Pumpkins giggle as they roll around,
Bananas do splits, oh how they astound!

A basket brims with joy and cheer,
Every munch whispers sweet things in your ear.
Grapes that dance in clusters so sly,
Raspberry giggles as they wave goodbye!

Tart apples prance in a playful race,
Strawberries wink with a cheeky face.
Berries in hats with sprinkles on top,
Harvesting giggles, we just can't stop!

Jump in the patch, let's have a blast,
With fruity delights, we're having a blast.
Each bite a chuckle, each sip a jest,
Off we go, in joy, we invest!

Sucrose Dreams

In a world where sugar rules supreme,
Syrupy rivers flow, a sweetened dream.
Chocolate chip cookies giggle at me,
Their gooey joy tastes like a jubilee!

Ice cream cones dance, a twirl in the sun,
Each flavor a laugh, a jolly good fun.
Sugar plums prance in a wild parade,
With frosting fireworks that never fade!

Bubbles of soda pop with fizz and cheer,
Jell-O jiggles, oh my, what a sphere!
Cotton candy wishes float in the breeze,
As sweet little smiles bring us to our knees!

So let's bounce on clouds of fluffy delight,
With giggles and snacks, we party all night.
In this sugary wonderland, dreams collide,
With every bite, let silliness abide!

Delirium of Fruity Fantasies

In a land where bananas ride bikes,
Pineapples wear hats, and call out hikes.
Melons with smiles, in jolly parade,
Laughing and giggling, they dance unafraid.

Grapes throw a party, they pop and they squish,
Jellybeans bounce in a rainbow fish.
A citrusy jester plays tricks outta sight,
While cherries roll dice under neon light.

The lemons all sing, with zest and with zeal,
Sipping on sunshine, oh what a meal!
In this fruity carnival, joy takes the lead,
Sipping on laughter, just follow the seed.

So come take a ride on this berry delight,
Where every bite's funny, and dreams take flight.
In the delirium of fruit, the sweet life begins,
With giggles and wiggles, and wide, grinning chins.

The Sugar-Coated Horizon

Look at that horizon, sweet like a dream,
Cotton candy clouds with a sugary theme.
Candy canes growing like trees everywhere,
Lollipops twirl in the warm, summer air.

A cupcake sun rises, all frosted and bright,
Doughnut-shaped mountains are quite a sight.
Marshmallow fluff fills the valleys below,
While gummy bears lead an energetic show.

Soda pop rain falls, with a fizzy surprise,
Slurping it up while we laugh till we cry.
Chocolate chip laughter, it sparkles and gleams,
In this sweet wonderland, we feast on our dreams.

So grab a balloon filled with sweetened delight,
As the sugar-coated horizon calls us tonight.
In a world spun from frolic, chance to explore,
The giggles and grins, who could ask for more?

Sweet Rainfall on Lips

When the clouds burst open with sweet, juicy drops,
Dancing on rooftops and sliding on tops.
A drizzle of soda, a sprinkle of cheer,
Bubbling up giggles when friends are near.

Strawberry showers and orange blurbs flow,
Ice cream cones blossom, making smiles glow.
Each raindrop a treat, like a candy parade,
With chocolate drizzle, oh what a cascade!

Catch the flavor bursts in the air, what a thrill,
As we twirl through puddles and roll down the hill.
The laughter erupts like a fizzy delight,
In this rain of confection, we dance through the night.

So let's open our mouths and savor the fun,
As we dash through the sweetness under warm, golden sun.
With a hop and a skip, and a plateful of chips,
Here's to a sprinkle of joy on our lips!

Harvesting Honeyed Dreams

In the garden of giggles, where dreams grow tall,
We gather the sweetness, come one, come all.
Honeybees buzzing, they dance with delight,
Filling the jars with joy, oh what a sight!

Plucking up dreams with a chuckle and cheer,
Giggling too loudly, can you hear?
Whisking up wishes like cakes in the air,
Frosted with laughter, shared everywhere.

A bumble of banter, a buzz so divine,
Let's toast with our cups, filled with sweetened wine.
In a frenzy of flavors, let's raise up our glee,
Harvesting moments, so wild and so free.

So plant a few seeds of giggles today,
Watch honeyed dreams bloom in the silliest way.
Gather around, friends, it's time to partake,
In the harvest of laughter, oh make no mistake!

A Dance of Flavor

In the jar, they tumble, oh what a sight,
Gummy bears waltzing, in colors so bright.
Chocolate chips groove, they jump and they sway,
Candy confetti just can't wait to play.

Marshmallows twirl, fluffy and round,
Licorice laces make a loop-de-loop sound.
Peppermint patties do a silly jig,
Jellybeans hip-hop, oh my, how they dig!

Soda pop fizzles like laughter in air,
Sugar sprinkles shower, without a care.
Lollipops spin, as if in a race,
With every flavor, it's a candy embrace.

So grab a sweet buddy, don't you be shy,
Let's dance with the treats, under candy skies.
A shimmy and shake, let happiness flow,
In this flavor dance, let the good times grow.

Sweets of the Earth

On a sunny day, under a gumdrop tree,
Lollipops whisper, 'Come climb here with me.'
Chocolate rivers flow past marshmallow hills,
Join in the laughter, surrender to thrills.

Candy corn critters are running around,
Their jellybean laughter is the happiest sound.
Gummy worms giggle, they wiggle and squirm,
While cookie crickets take turns to confirm.

Cupcake clouds float in bubblegum skies,
With frosting rainbows that catch our eyes.
Honey drips softly from honeycomb charms,
A sweetness that wraps us in warm, gentle arms.

Let's make a picnic, spread treats on the grass,
With laughter and joy, let the moments surpass.
Each sugary morsel a secret delight,
In a land full of giggles, everything feels right.

Glimmers of Sugar

Under the sun, we gather to munch,
Marbled macarons make for a fun brunch.
Sprinkles are twinkling like stars in a show,
Sugar plums dancing, putting on a glow.

Cotton candy castles rise high in the air,
With giggly marshmallows, not a worry or care.
Frosty ice cream cones tip over with style,
Each cone a comedian, making us smile.

Toffee pops giggle, in flavors they boast,
While licorice ropes playfully tease the toast.
Sundae sherbet spins, a colorful blend,
In this comical feast, where sweetness won't end.

So grab a big spoon, and let's not be shy,
In this sugar-coated dreamland, we soar high.
With every last bite, let the laughter expand,
For nothing's more funny than treats that are grand.

The Essence of Joy

A cupcake pipeline runs wild through the town,
Where frosting flows freely, no need for a frown.
Caramels giggle from high up on the shelf,
'Join in the fun!' they yell, 'Be yourself!'

Popcorn kernels jive, and candy corn sings,
Licorice laughter, oh, what joy it brings!
Soda bubbles burst, like fireworks of cheer,
With every sweet noise, the fun's crystal clear.

Banana peels slip in a comical dance,
As chocolate fountains give laughter a chance.
Marshmallows launch from this giggle brigade,
Creating a carnival, sweet parade.

So let us rejoice, with each sugary bite,
In this land of delight, happiness takes flight.
With laughter our anthem, and candies our prize,
With joy in our hearts, we'll reach for the skies.

Palette of Elysian Flavors

Upon my tongue a circus, oh what a show,
Lemon drops and cherry bombs all in a row.
Caramel rivers flowing down my chin,
I laugh as the sugar rush begins to spin.

A pickle does the tango with a piece of cheese,
Chocolate-covered crickets dance with ease.
The waltz of custard, oh what a display,
Fruits in the spotlight, all here to play.

Marshmallow clouds float on pudding streams,
Gummy bears whisper all my sweet dreams.
Cotton candy flows like a whimsical breeze,
With flavors so silly, it's sure to please.

Lollipop lovers, raise your toast!
To flavors so wild, let's all brag and boast.
With every bite laughter bubbles and gleams,
In this silly palace, we feast on our dreams.

Serenade of Sweet Blossoms

Honey drips, and sugar sings, oh what a song,
Cupcake fairies laughing, they all belong.
Blueberry bushes share a winking jest,
While marshmallow rabbits invite you for a fest.

Jellybean jesters jump from the fridge,
In a candy parade, let's make a bridge.
Pies do the cha-cha, with crusts crisp and light,
Who knew dessert could stir such delight?

Fizzy soda bubbles tease with a spritz,
A chocolate fountain does an acrobatic split.
Gingerbread giants stumble and trip,
While caramel kangaroos share a sweet sip.

So gather your pals for this sugary ride,
With giggles and flavors, let laughter be our guide.
In the garden of sweetness, where joy is our key,
Savor the silliness, come dance with me!

The Ambrosial Journey

Off we go on a flavor quest, oh what fun,
Picking peach petals under the sun.
Lemonade lakes where popsicle boats roam,
Every sip a giggle, it feels like home.

Marzipan mountains with gummy bear peaks,
We plod through pudding, all giggles and squeaks.
Chocolate chip cookies wave from the shore,
Into this frolic, let's leap and explore.

Cupcakes in hats, they nod to my dance,
Donuts in tutus give me a chance.
Swirls of whipped cream, all fluffy and bright,
Got a spoonful of joy, let's taste the delight.

So here on this journey, my friends, take a spoon,
With laughter and flavors, we'll be there soon.
A sprinkle of magic, a pinch of sublime,
Join in this fun, it's our glorious time!

Essence of a Joyful Harvest

Pick strawberries ripe for a pancake fest,
With maple syrup smiles, we're feeling blessed.
Oven-baked giggles come bubbling alive,
As sugar coats laughter, we all will thrive.

Peach cobbler moons shine in the night,
While pies do a jig, oh what a sight!
Each slice brings a chuckle, each fork a cheer,
With desserts like these, there's nothing to fear.

The corn on the cob dances with sass,
While broccoli prances, 'Don't let me pass!'
Veggies unite in this joyful parade,
With buttery smiles, their fears allayed.

So let's harvest laughter, and share every bite,
With quirky flavors, let's take to flight.
In the fields of sweet whimsy, let's gather around,
For joy in each morsel, let's spread it all around.

Delightful Nectar

In a world of candy rain,
A squirrel steals my lollipop.
He grins with a sugary stain,
I laugh as he makes his hop.

Chocolate rivers flow and swirl,
I built a bridge from chewy gum.
Beneath the candy cotton curl,
Gumdrops dance, oh what a hum!

Licorice twists like a dancer's shoe,
Marshmallow clouds bounce all around.
I trip on taffy, wouldn't you?
But laughter's worth the sticky ground.

Jellybeans play a game of tag,
While lollipops watch from afar.
I chase them down, pull out a rag,
This mess, I swear, is quite bizarre!

Savoring Sunlit Moments

In a park where bubbles soar,
Ice cream drips on my new shirt.
Kids giggle, rolling on the floor,
While I pretend to be a dessert.

Lemon drops fall from the sky,
Splashing sweet on my lemonade.
I take a sip with a sly eye,
Soon there's no more drink to aid.

Sunshine sprinkles in my hair,
Like powdered sugar on a cake.
I dance and twirl without a care,
In this moment, my heart's awake.

A puppy steals my cookie treat,
His wagging tail gets all the blame.
As crumbs fly from his happy feat,
I laugh, it's all part of the game!

The Honeyed Whisper

Whispers of bees buzz through the air,
As I chase honey on a spoon.
It's got me dancing in my chair,
The sweetness makes me sing a tune.

Crumpets piled high with jam and cheer,
Every bite's a laughing prank.
Squished strawberries try to disappear,
But I'm too busy, oh how I thank!

A generous swirl on my cheek,
Sugar ants march in a parade.
I give a wink to the cheeky freak,
Their tiny feet can't invade!

At dusk, I sip my golden tea,
With lemon dancing on the rim.
The honey laughs along with me,
Each sip's a little wild whim!

A Symphony of Sugared Dreams

In a land where cupcakes sing,
Frosting notes tumble and twirl.
Gummy bears wear bling-bling,
As jellybeans begin to whirl.

A taffy whale leaps with a splash,
While licorice waves swirl with flair.
Chocolate fountains make quite a crash,
In this land of candied air.

Dancing donuts spin round and round,
Their sprinkles shower the glee.
I catch a flake that I have found,
Oh how sweet this life could be!

With every bite, laughter's the song,
In this orchestra of delight.
Where every flavor sings along,
And dreams are sprinkled just right!

The Taste of Sunshine on My Soul

A lemon drop fell from the sky,
I caught it quick, oh my, oh my!
With every bite, my worries flee,
Sunshine giggles inside of me.

Chocolate rivers, oh what a sight,
Marshmallow clouds in the warm daylight.
Candy corn sprouted from my shoe,
Who knew that slipping could taste so new?

A popsicle dance upon my tongue,
It jiggled and jangled, sweetly sung.
In laughter's arms, all frowns combust,
This sugary world? It's a must!

Gummy bears prance, so round and bright,
In this candy land, all feels just right.
With sprinkles raining, I twirl and sway,
Sunshine smiles at me all day!

Blissful Cravings Entwined

In a cupcake forest, I boldly roam,
My heart is flickering like candy chrome.
Frosting rivers, oh what a mess,
But who cares when I can digress?

A jellybean parade marches by,
While licorice vines reach for the sky.
Bouncing berry bushes, oh what fun,
It feels like I'm laughing with everyone!

Soda pop rain falls from above,
The fizzy splash, it fits like a glove.
Unicorns dance to the bubble tune,
Sipping on smiles beneath the moon.

Chocolate chip stars twinkle in sight,
I gobble them up with sheer delight.
Life is a party, each flavor divine,
In this sugary realm, I forever shine!

Savoring Nectar

A honey bee flew in for a chat,
Said, 'Life's too short, let's have a snack!'
With nectar dreams swirling all around,
We laughed and danced on the sugar ground.

Fruit loops echoed a joyous tune,
I juggled oranges under the moon.
Pineapple swings, what a wild ride,
With laughter and sweetness by my side.

Marshmallow hats on friends so dear,
In a world of treats, it's all sincere.
Bubbles of giggles, the joy spills forth,
This whimsical place is a candy worth.

Each fruit slice sparkling with delight,
We toast with cupcakes, oh what a sight!
In the nectar's glow, we twirl and play,
Savoring joy in the best of ways!

The Sugar of Life

A cherry on top, life's little flair,
Made for mishaps and jokes to share.
With frosting fingers and silly grins,
We chase the sweetness that always wins.

Cotton candy clouds float on by,
Smiles stick like gum, oh me, oh my!
I stumbled on sugar, tripped on the fun,
In this candy chaos, I've truly run.

Ice cream mountains that melt away,
We navigate sprinkles in joyful play.
Each scoop a giggle, each cone a cheer,
In this sugary dream, there's never fear.

Life is a cupcake, frosted and round,
Take a big bite, let laughter abound.
With laughter's whisk, and joy's sweet knife,
We slice and serve the sugar of life!

Sweets Woven in Sunlight

In a kitchen where giggles arise,
Flour flies high, oh what a surprise!
Cookies dance like they're in a race,
Chocolate chips jump, pure pastry grace.

Whisking up dreams, we apply the heat,
Baking's a game, who can resist the treat?
Lollipop towers, we build to the sky,
Icing cascades like it's happy to fly.

Sprinkle a rainbow on cakes that we bake,
Frosting fights back with each little shake.
Giggles explode as we taste test a bit,
Swapping our spoons, we're never done with it!

So, grab a cupcake, let's join in the fun,
Life is a feast, get ready to run!
With laughter and sweets, we'll savor the night,
In this sugary world, everything's bright!

Caressing the Savor

Pies cooling gently on the windowsill,
The aroma of sugar gives quite a thrill.
With forks in our hands, we make quite the scene,
Devouring dessert like a horde of caffeine!

Marshmallows roast near a crackling flame,
Bites of delight are the ones we all claim.
S'mores in the making, gooey and grand,
Where laughter erupts, and marshmallows stand.

Taste buds are dancing, a whimsical jig,
Eating the frosting—oh, it's time to dig!
Sugar-fueled gossip with friends at the table,
Happiness comes in a colorful label.

So let's eat our fill, make no fuss or fuss,
Join in the laughter, come on, let's discuss!
In this sweet sanctuary, we're free as a dove,
Savoring the joy, it's a treat we all love!

Delightful Crescendo

Cake layers stacked in a towering show,
Slathered with frosting, oh what a glow!
Each slice brings giggles, a sweet serenade,
With sprinkles that shimmer, our worries all fade.

Lemon drops tumble, a zesty parade,
Candy clouds drifting, sweet dreams they've made.
Popsicles melting, a summer affair,
Slurping and laughing without a care!

Fruit salad parties with colors that bribe,
Chewing our fruit bites, we dance and we vibe.
Sassy gummy bears wiggle and jive,
In this sugary jungle, we're so glad we thrive!

So, gather your spoons, it's time to delight,
With giggles and sweets, we'll party all night!
In a cheerful crescendo, our laughter will soar,
Together we feast, and who could ask for more?

Mirthful Bites

Nibbles of joy on a bright sunny day,
Cookies that crumble just right on the tray.
Cupcake concoctions with sprinkles galore,
One bite and you'll wish for just one bite more!

Fudge that winks from a glistening plate,
Goodness and giggles, the fun's never late.
Baking mishaps lead to mouth-watering sights,
Flour fights follow, oh what sweet delights!

Candy canes tumble amidst frosty cheer,
Chomp on the sweetness, it's time to draw near.
With chocolate fountains, we'll dive in with glee,
Sticky and silly, it's a treat jubilee!

So huddle together for mirthful bites,
Where joy meets dessert under sparkling lights!
In laughter and sweetness, the world feels just right,
With morsels of magic, let's savor the night!

Lush Fields of Dessert Dreams

In fields of cream and whipped delight,
I chase the pies in silly flight.
With every slice I take a leap,
Beware the crumbs, they make me weep.

The chocolate rivers flow so wide,
I paddle through on doughnut tide.
A marshmallow tree, oh what a sight,
I bounce on puffs, it feels just right!

Sundae mountains, cone-topped peaks,
Where gummy bears will play hide and seeks.
I laugh so hard, I start to roll,
In this dessert-filled, joyous stroll.

So join the feast, don't be a bore,
We'll giggle as we crave some more.
With every giggle, flavor blooms,
In lush dessert fields where joy resumes.

Melodies of Sugared Days

A symphony of glazes bright,
Sugar plums dance, oh what a sight!
Lollipops twirl in a sugary breeze,
As gummy worms wiggle with ease.

I sing with cakes in playful tunes,
Whipped cream clouds float under moons.
Candied apples, a crunchy beat,
I jiggle and jive, feel the sweet heat!

Cookies clap with chocolate cheers,
While jellybeans giggle through the years.
In marshmallow harmony, we unite,
A funny feast that feels just right.

With sprinkles raining from above,
Each note is laced with sugar love.
Come join this fun, let laughter sway,
In melodies of our sugared day.

A Cornucopia of Glee

In baskets stacked with frosted treats,
Pies and cakes form tasty feats.
I dive into a donut pit,
With cream-filled joy, I wildly fit.

A fruit parade, oh what a scene,
Bananas and berries in a jolly sheen.
Unicorn cupcakes with glittering swirls,
Giggles fly like spinning twirls.

Cotton candy clouds float on by,
As gummy fish swim in the sky.
Wobbling jello makes me grin,
In this cornucopia, let's begin!

Each bite brings laughter, so divine,
Share a laugh over candied vine.
A feast of fun, oh can't you see?
This joyful platter brings us glee!

Dreaming in Cotton Candy Skies

In skies of fluff, I drift away,
On clouds of sweet, I'll laugh and play.
Marzipan stars twinkle so bright,
As I bounce on gumdrops, pure delight!

I soar through dreams on sugar wings,
To taste the joy that laughter brings.
With chocolate rains and candy trees,
Life's a joke, oh pass the peas!

Soda fountains burst in giggles sweet,
As candied critters dance on their feet.
In every flavor, a chuckle hides,
Beneath the cream, the fun abides.

So join my flight in whims so grand,
Where goofy sweets are close at hand.
In cotton candy dreams we'll glide,
Laughter our compass, joy our guide.

Carnival of Flavors

The jellybeans jump, they dance all around,
Chocolate pretzels make the silliest sound.
Cotton candy clouds float high in the sky,
While licorice snakes slither and sigh.

Sour gummies giggle, they're having a ball,
Marshmallow peeps bounce and tumble, then fall.
A parade of flavors goes zipping on through,
Even the popcorn is sharing its brew.

With caramel drizzles making a splash,
The toffee is busy with quite a bash.
Honeycomb giggles, so sweet and so bright,
In this flavor carnival, everything's light!

Round and round here, we keep spinning sweets,
Every small bite comes with whimsical treats.
Lollipops cheer, while cupcakes do the twist,
In this wacky fair, who could resist?

Shimmering Sweets

Fizzy drinks dance in a rainbow parade,
Cookies in costumes are all homemade.
The chocolate chip pirate sails on a sea,
With peanut butter treasures, it's funny, you see!

Marshmallows twirl in a frosting delight,
Sparkling sugar sprinkles take flight in the night.
Jelly is wiggling, it jests and it jabs,
While cupcakes in hats throw hilarious jabs.

Gummy bears giggle, they jive and they sway,
While taffy gets tangled in a silly ballet.
The licorice band plays a tune full of cheer,
In a world full of sweetness, there's nothing to fear.

Shimmering sweets with a wink and a nod,
Bake some fun munchies, my sweet little odd.
Join in the laughter; it's all understood,
In the land of desserts, it's all pretty good!

Fruitful Whims

A pineapple juggles with oranges nearby,
While cherries wear hats as they wave and they fly.
Bananas slip past with a curve in their grin,
In this fruity festival, let the fun begin!

Lemons are laughing with zest in the air,
Grapes play hide and seek without any care.
Each berry's a joker, plotting their schemes,
In the land of fruitiness, anything seems!

Watermelons roll with a splat and a splish,
Mangoes make music, oh, what a sweet dish!
Kiwi takes center stage, it's all quite absurd,
As apples recite lines, it's truly unheard!

Fruits bounce in harmony, each flavor a joke,
With fruity fun antics, the apples provoke.
There's magic in laughter, it bubbles and gleams,
In the world of whims, we savor our dreams!

Subtle Pleasures

A cupcake whispers secrets, its frosting so sly,
Donuts make faces, oh me, oh my!
Brownies are plotting with fudge on the sly,
While cookies are giggling, oh my, oh my!

Cinnamon swirls lead a subtle parade,
Pies twirl in circles, their crust is displayed.
Whipped cream stands tall with a hint of a wink,
While the cookies all whisper, let us not sink!

Truffles are teasing with flavors galore,
Marzipan shapes knock on fudge-coated doors.
Each morsel is chuckling beneath the soft light,
In this realm of delight, everything's bright!

So grab a small taste of each little treasure,
Every sweet bite brings untold pleasure.
In the land of desserts, there's giggles galore,
With subtle sweet wonders, who could ask for more?

Honeyed Whispers

In the jar, a sticky thrill,
Bumblebees have had their fill.
Spoon in hand, I dive right in,
Can't resist, let the fun begin!

Golden drips on pancakes stack,
Oh dear, now there's sauce on my back.
Laughter echoes, syrup slips,
Breakfast dance with honeyed trips.

A buzzing chorus fills the air,
Dripping sweetness everywhere.
Taste the giggles, savor the joke,
Honey glues the morning folk!

So grab your forks, let's make a mess,
Life is sweeter, I must confess.
With every bite, joy-filled and loud,
In this sticky fun, we're all so proud!

Delight on the Tongue

Wobbling jelly, wiggle and sway,
I dare to taste, come what may!
Gummy bears in a sugar rush,
My tongue's in a playful, dizzy hush.

Lollipop lady, oh what a sight,
Her rainbow stash, pure delight!
Circle and twirl, flavors collide,
In this sugary ride, there's nowhere to hide.

Chocolate fountains, a drippy scheme,
Dunk my face, oh, what a dream!
Laughter erupts, sweet chaos reigns,
Sticky fingers, fun remains.

With every nibble, joy does bloom,
Candy carnival in every room.
So grab a sweet and join my spree,
In this flavor circus, come laugh with me!

A Symphony of Flavors

A bang, a sip, what's that taste?
Fragrant fruits, nothing goes to waste.
Pineapple trumpet, blueberry drum,
Taste buds laughing, oh, how they hum!

Citrus zing in a fizzy whirl,
Spinning flavors make my head twirl.
With each note, the laughter rings,
Join the choir, and dance with kings!

Marshmallow clouds floating so high,
What's that? A caramel pie in the sky!
Skipping through sugar, I hit the floor,
Every bite creates laughter and more.

So raise a glass of fizzy cheer,
Life's a joke filled with sweetened beer.
In this raucous tune, sip along,
Flavorful fun is where we belong!

Sip of Elysium

With a slurp, it spills and splashes,
Cool and fruity, life dashes!
Smoothies swirl, a colorful dream,
Laughter bubbles, bursting at the seam.

Ice cream towers, oh so grand,
Blow a bubble, with sticky hand!
Sundae giggles topped with sprinkles,
In sweet delight, my heart crinkles.

Slurping loudly, no shame around,
Cherries toppled without a sound.
Giggles mix with chocolaty bliss,
This is the moment I cannot miss!

Sip after sip, the joy overflows,
Taste on laughter, how brightly it glows!
In this creamy world of fun and glee,
Every sip is pure jubilee!

Bursting with Golden Juices

Juice drips down like rain from the sky,
I thought I'd sip, but it jumped, oh my!
The apples giggle, the pears do a dance,
A fountain of flavor in a wild romance.

Lemons make faces, a squirt on my nose,
Berries are winking, it's quite the show!
I grab a big bunch, ready to munch,
But one slipped away—oh, what a crunch!

Cherries are laughing, bright red on the tree,
As I reach for a handful, they say, "Not for thee!"
Plums stand in line for a juicy parade,
Only to burst in a fruity charade.

So if you should wander among the fruit stand,
Beware of the splashes and sticky hand brand!
Each drop is a plunge into sweet, silly might,
A carnival party, a sugary fight!

The Honeycomb's Embrace

Buzzing along with a sticky sweet tune,
The bees do a jig, under light of the moon.
A hive full of giggles, a whirl of delight,
Each drop of the nectar feels oh-so-right.

With a spoon in hand, I felt like a king,
The golden goo swirls, it's a glorious thing!
But the bees rolled their eyes, said, "Hey, that's our stash,

You've got to share more or we'll give you a splash!"

So I danced with the bees, under honey-dripped trees,
Finding sweet joy in the buzz of the breeze.
With laughter and puns, we created a scene,
A sticky affair that was fit for a queen!

Who knew that a pot could be such a delight?
A sweetened connection, a whimsical rite.
So comes my lesson from this buzz-filled embrace,
Never take honey without bringing some grace!

Caramel Kisses at Twilight

Under the stars, the caramels glisten,
I lean in close, oh, how they do whisper!
With a wink and a smile, they beckon my way,
A squirty surprise for a sweet tooth at play.

The drizzle of sweetness flows down from above,
Like candy-coated dreams wrapped in love.
With chocolate companions, they form quite a pack,
Together they bounce, with a sticky attack.

On marshmallow clouds, we rise and we glide,
With fudgy surprises, we wave and we ride.
Each twinkling bite, what a comical treat,
As laughter erupts, oh, the joy is complete!

So gather your friends and look to the skies,
For caramel kisses are quite the surprise!
In this twilight wonder, we'll savor the night,
With giggles and laughter—it feels just right!

A Dance of Syrupy Delights

Maple syrup flowed, a river in sight,
I grabbed my big pancake, oh what a bite!
But it wiggled away, like a slippery fish,
"Oh pancake," I laughed, "you're my scrumptious wish!"

Waffles waved back, said, "We're here for a dance,
With honey on top, we'll give joy a chance!"
Fluffy and fluffy, they bounce all around,
A syrupy festival, pure sweetness abound.

The toast made a joke, "I'm a buttered delight!"
As we dipped and we twirled in this sugary night.
The sweetness was thick, and I couldn't resist,
A giggle and munch, getting lost in the mist.

So come one, come all, to this syrupy spree,
Embrace the delights, just you wait and see!
With laughter and sugar, we'll twirl in the gleam,
In this sticky adventure, we're living the dream!

Twinkling Sweet Meditations

I pondered chocolate on a bright sunny day,
Imagining candies would come out to play.
The jellybeans danced with a sugary flair,
While bananas in pajamas sang tunes in the air.

Pies flew by on a sparkle-filled breeze,
Pie crust and whipped cream brought me to my knees.
A gummy bear serenade, what a delight,
As marshmallows moonwalked throughout the night.

Silken Essence of Delight

In a land where cupcakes wear sparkly hats,
And ice cream cones chatter with fluffy green cats.
The lollipops giggle, that's quite a scene,
As gumdrops play hide-and-seek on the green.

A soda pop fountain with bubbles so bright,
Poured laughter and joy from morning to night.
Chocolate fountains cascade without care,
While licorice vines twirl in the warm air.

A Garden of Sugary Treasures

In a garden where lollies bloom like a rose,
With candy canes growing, as everyone knows.
The sour patch kids come to play with delight,
In a gummy worm dance party that lasts through the night.

Chocolate bunnies hop in a marshmallow field,
With soft sugary clouds that happily yield.
Licorice vines tangle and sweeten the air,
As jellybean fairies twirl without care.

Sweet Pairs and Dreamy Flavors

Chocolate and peanut butter are best friends you see,
They giggle and play in a dance with a spree.
Strawberry and cream shared a whimsical jest,
While sprinkles on top wore their colors the best.

Mint and chocolate joined in a wild pirouette,
As caramel's laughter was hard to forget.
Cupcake and cookie sang songs of delight,
In a whirl of sweet flavors that danced through the night.

The Orchard's Hidden Treasure

In the orchard, smiles abound,
Lost where juicy secrets are found.
Pears giggle, apples roll,
Cherries dance with a happy soul.

Beneath the tree, a picnic laid,
With fruits of laughter, no need for shade.
Munching mangoes, sticky hands,
Creating messes, just like we planned.

The squirrels stare, they want in too,
On this feast, they smell the brew.
Lemons bounce in a game of catch,
While we giggle, the moments match.

In this treasure, playful bites,
Life's a feast, with pure delights.
Orchard whispers, "Come have fun!"
Each sweet joy feels like a pun.

Whispers of Fruity Bliss

In the basket, fruits conspire,
Whispers of sweetness do not tire.
Bananas joke, they slip and slide,
Mischievous zest, how they divide!

Peaches prance with a fuzzy flair,
Ripe laughter fills the summer air.
Blueberries burst in tiny glee,
"Come join our jam, oh won't you see?"

Grapes are rolling, playing chase,
A fruity showdown, a silly race.
Even lemons sing a tune,
Making jokes 'neath the bright full moon.

In this garden of fun and cheer,
Joyful bites are always near.
Each fruit a smile, each laugh a spark,
Sweetness found, like a jest in the dark.

Sweet Threads of Time

Each fruit a thread in time's great quilt,
Stitched in laughter, with joy we built.
Time hops like a silly sprout,
With nectarous tales that never pout.

Crisp apples tell of days gone by,
While lemons joke with a zesty sigh.
Melons mimic their watermelon kin,
All bursting forth with a cheeky grin.

Berries blush in a sunlit glow,
Tickling taste buds, putting on a show.
Slice up laughter, season with cheer,
Moments sweet, like the fruits we steer.

Tangled love in a fruity dance,
Each bite a jester's bold romance.
Time sips nectar, oh what a delight,
In this fruity world, we take flight.

Revelry in Sugary Rain

Like candy canes in a playful storm,
Sugar droplets that twist and swarm.
Lemons giggle, they chuckle in bliss,
As lollipops join in a fruity kiss.

Rain of sweetness, where laughter pours,
Munching gumballs, we dance on floors.
Bubblegum clouds float high above,
Sprinkling joy, like candy love.

Cotton candy, a swirling whirl,
Silly faces make our heads twirl.
With every splash, a joke anew,
In this party, we all imbue.

The storm rolls on, but we won't frown,
In sugary rain, we never drown.
Just sweet delight, in this playful game,
Fruity laughter, our hearts aflame.

The Secret of Confection

In a world made of chocolate, oh what a sight,
Where candy canes twirl on a frosty night.
Marshmallow clouds float on a jellybean sky,
And gummy bears giggle as they bounce by.

Fudge rivers flow with a caramel breeze,
Sprinkled with laughter like confetti from trees.
Lollipops gossip about the flavor chase,
While donut holes wiggle in a sugary race.

A cupcake confesses to a pie in a grin,
"Your crust is so flaky, let's spin and begin!"
With frosting as hats, the sweets dance around,
In a sugar-filled party where joy knows no bounds.

So here is the secret, if you dare to believe:
Life tastes much sweeter when you let yourself weave.
Find joy in the nibble, embrace every bite,
And laugh with the candies under the moonlight.

Lush Landscapes of Flavor

In a meadow where strawberries twirl in delight,
Blueberries giggle, a most charming sight.
Cotton candy clouds, oh what a hue,
Rain down with sprinkles in a bright sugary view.

There's a licorice river, oh how it flows,
With marshmallow rocks where the gumdrops grow.
Every fruit whispers secrets of taste,
While cookies and brownies perform with no haste.

Fountains of soda bubble with glee,
As popcorn kernels pop with a jubilant spree.
Beneath gummy trees, laughter does ring,
In this fruitful paradise, joy takes to wing.

So wander the pathways, let flavors ignite,
In this land of munchables, everything's right.
With giggles and grins, we frolic and prance,
In a lush landscape where we all do a dance.

Pearls of Pudding

In a bowl of delight, the pudding does gleam,
A treasure of flavors, sweet as a dream.
Chocolate jewels sparkle, oh what a treat,
While jellybeans jive to a sugary beat.

Meringue clouds fluff up their powdered wigs,
As caramel whirlwinds perform little jigs.
Baked Alaska shivers at the marshmallow sun,
While whipped cream sails in, bringing giggles and fun.

Cookie crumbles tumble in layers so neat,
As syrup rivers flow with a bubbly tweet.
Ice cream cones wobble, their hats in a spin,
Feeling quite dapper in the dessert din.

So gather your spoons, let's dig in with cheer,
For pearls of pudding bring laughter near.
With every sweet scoop, let worries take flight,
In a world made of flavors, everything's bright.

Sweetest Embrace

In the cozy corner of a candy-filled lair,
Chocolate hugs licorice without any care.
Lollipops giggle, they dance and they sway,
While jellybeans jump in a playful display.

Under marshmallow blankets, the pastries unite,
Chanting berry lullabies into the night.
Frosting embraces all with a warm, sticky kiss,
A sweetness so grand, it feels like pure bliss.

Ring in the giggles, let laughter expand,
Life's a dessert that's perfectly planned.
Gummy worms wiggle, all ready to shimmy,
In this sweetest embrace, nothing feels grimy.

So when you feel glum, just look to the treat,
Embrace all the flavors, hear the laughter repeat.
With each scoop of joy, let the giggles unfurl,
In a world full of sweets, it's a candy-coated swirl.

The Drawing of Delight

Oh, chocolate cake, oh fudge surprise,
With icing dreams that dance and rise.
A nibble here, a bite or two,
I'm feeling fine, I've found my crew.

Whipped cream clouds upon my pie,
I laugh and giggle, oh my, oh my!
Each forkful flings a sugar spree,
My pants scream tight, oh joy to be!

Cookies crumble, laughter flies,
With sprinkles twinkling in our eyes.
A pastry party, oh the thrill,
I'll take the last, oh what a skill!

In this dessert, we bond and grow,
Giggles rise like frothy dough.
With every bite, the world is bright,
I'll do it all again tonight!

Craving the Divine

A donut dunked in coffee bliss,
Is there a sweeter way than this?
Sprinkled dreams and frosted hope,
My heart is dancing with each scope.

Cupcakes tower like a grand parade,
A cherry on top, a masterpiece made.
I'm plotting schemes for one more bite,
With frosting battles, we laugh all night.

With pastries spinning like a wheel,
I wave the diet, here's the deal!
Let's trade our worries for layers sweet,
A snack attack that can't be beat!

When joy is piled high like cream,
In sugar dreams, we all can scheme.
We'll laugh till crumbs are all you see,
In our sweet world, forever free!

Laced with Honey

Oh honey drizzled on my bread,
With nutty friends, joy's easily spread.
A giggle here, a sticky sight,
My fingers dance in pure delight.

Peanut butter, thick and bold,
A lunchtime story yet untold.
With every scoop, I start to grin,
This flavor war is sure to win!

Jelly jiggles, a wobbling treat,
On crackers, it can't be beat.
A bite and laugh, it never fails,
As sweetness drips and laughter sails!

With syrup swirling, a breakfast cheer,
Pancakes stacked like love sincere.
In every drop, a jiggle and clap,
Let's hold this moment, take a nap!

The Richness of Bloom

Garden fruits in colors bright,
A splash of berries, what a sight!
With laughter bubbling like a brew,
Each bite brings joy, oh so true.

Watermelons roll, a summer fling,
I toss one high, the laughter's king.
Bananas split with giggles near,
Who knew fruit could bring such cheer?

Pineapples dance in tropical heat,
Where fruity tales and laughter meet.
A party fruit salad, quite a spread,
We dive right in, no need for dread!

Let's crunch and munch through every meal,
In gardens wild, our hearts can heal.
With sweetness blooming, joy's in the air,
A feast for all, we've found our flare!

Golden Moments of Indulgence

In a world where candy rains,
I chase chocolate without any reins.
Gummy bears stick to my shoes,
Oh, the sweet life, one can't refuse!

Soda fountains drip like a dream,
Marshmallow clouds—what a theme!
Lollipops dancing on the street,
Join the parade of sugary feet!

Cookies wink from their glassy shelves,
They know how to tease all the elves.
Accidental frosting on my nose,
Naughty giggles, the mischief grows!

So let's skip, and twirl in delight,
Where all desserts are just out of sight.
In this kingdom of all things sweet,
Let's munch and crunch, and never retreat!

Layers of Cherry Bliss

In a pie stacked high with a cherry crown,
I dive right in, never wearing a frown.
Spoonfuls of laughter, whipped cream on top,
Each bite a giggle, can't help but hop!

Jelly donuts with powdered snow,
Take one big bite, and watch the show!
Sprinkle wars on the kitchen floor,
A taste explosion—who could ask for more?

Chocolate drips on my favorite shirt,
Oops! Sweet chaos, ah, what a dessert!
With flavors swirling like a dance,
Each new bite gives the tongue a chance!

Cupcakes with sprinkles like confetti rain,
Life's little joys, joy without pain.
I'll eat them all, then run a mile,
Sneaking one more, can't resist the style!

Velvet Fruits of Desire

Raspberry ribbons tied with care,
Soft and squishy, they lurk everywhere.
Fruit bowls winking, they call my name,
With every nibble, it's all just a game!

Bananas wearing spotted coats,
Each peel a ticket to sugary moats.
Peaches giggle with fuzzy delight,
One juicy bite feels oh so right!

Melon slices, the coolest of friends,
Playing dress-up, the fun never ends.
Wiggly jello, oh what a scene,
It's a fruit party, how sweet and serene!

So gather the gang, it's fruiting hour,
Let's toast to joy, with sugary power.
In this buffet of nature's best,
We'll munch and crunch—what a jest!

Flourish of Flavors

Ice cream towers built to the sky,
Screaming for joy, no need to be shy.
With sprinkles like stars on a big scoop mount,
I dive right in, oh what a bount!

Cupcakes twirl in glittery skirts,
My taste buds dance, oh how it flirts!
Frosting rivers—giddy and sweet,
Dripping with laughter from top to feet!

Fried dough whirls with sugary grace,
Powdered sugar fluffs on my face!
In a land where flavors all collide,
Every bite's a joyous joyride!

So bring on the party, let's have a blast,
With fields of flavors that are unsurpassed.
In the kingdom of treats, let giggles sing,
Sugar-coated dreams, oh what joys they bring!

www.ingramcontent.com/pod-product-compliance
Lightning Source LLC
Chambersburg PA
CBHW070003300426
43661CB00141B/154